Xenophobe's®
guide to the
ALBANIANS

Alan Andoni

GW00645132

Xenophobe's Guides

Published by Xenophobe's® Guides.

Telephone: +44 (0)20 7733 8585
E-mail: info@xenophobes.com
Web site: www.xenophobes.com

Published 2015

Editor – Catriona Tulloch Scott
Series Editor – Anne Tauté
Cover designer – Vicki Towers
Printer – CPI Antony Rowe, Wiltshire

Grateful thanks are given to Dr Robert Elsie
for his translation of the verse on page 35
from *Fshati im* by Andon Zako Çajupi
published in *Baba-Tomorri*, Cairo 1902.

Cover: Tribute for the mannequins in Albanian
costume is paid to Albaniaheritage.com.

ePub ISBN: 9781908120960
Mobi ISBN: 9781908120977
Print ISBN: 9781906042189

Contents

The population of Albania is just over 3 million, compared with 11 million Greeks, 61 million Italians, 63 million British and 318 million Americans.

Albania is a little bit bigger than Sicily, and could fit into France 20 times.

Nationalism & Identity

Pride and prejudice

Albanians will tell you that they are proud to be Albanians. What they won't tell you is why. Some will mention the national hero Skanderbeg, some the Illyrian tribes (from whom they are descended), some the language ('the oldest in Europe'), and some Mother Teresa (an ethnic Albanian). The remarkable landscape might also be mentioned. However, the plain fact is that nobody really knows.

On the other hand, they are aware of their reputation. Some are ready to describe themselves (or rather other Albanians) as lazy, corrupt, more interested in drinking coffee than working. Some present their country as spoilt, decaying and in disrepair – and their dream is to live outside the country. A common phrase is '*Shqiperia nuk behet me Shqiptare*', 'Albania cannot *become* [move ahead] with Albanians'.

> **❝A common phrase is 'Albania cannot *become* with Albanians'.❞**

The more insightful point out that the nation managed to maintain its language, culture and identity (albeit heavily influenced by outsiders) for two millennia, endured persistent invasions by its neighbours, and occupation and administration by the Ottoman Turks for up to five centuries. They can also cite the Albanians' ability to emerge after 40 years of the excesses of the communist regime and to survive under a succession of (it is said) inept, self-serving governments for a further 20. In the end, the flag of the black eagle on the red background and the national anthem (composed by a Romanian) give rise to a fulsome patriotism which galvanises a strong feeling of raw, unbridled pride that pays no heed to intellectual rationalisation. As in many nations, symbolic representations and slogans can eclipse meaningful thought.

History matters

If Albanians look to the future, it is to the immediate future for they have no faith in anything further ahead. As such, history plays a role in self-definition.

> **66 Albanians look to the immediate future for they have no faith in anything further ahead. 99**

In ancient times Albania was called Illyria and its tribes stretched as far north as present-day Slovenia. Though it has no counterpart today, the concept of Illyria is a cornerstone of identity for all Albanians, a large number of whom are located on its borders in Southern Montenegro, Western Macedonia, Northern Greece and in Kosovo where they form the majority ethnic group.

The Albanians' recent history is a little more

ambiguous. There is a general consensus that the communist era was bad – because it limited freedom, because the population couldn't travel abroad, and because people were sent to prison camps – though there is seldom any focus on detail. Albania is one of the few communist countries that (as yet) does not have a museum entirely dedicated to the victims of communism. The tangible legacy of the era is the concrete

> **❝ The house of the former dictator still stands as a triumph of conceit over aesthetics. ❞**

bunkers, 700,000 of which were built from 1967 until 1985; the intangible legacy is harder to assess. The house of the former dictator, the late and largely unlamented Enver Hoxha, still stands as a triumph of conceit over aesthetics in a corner of the 'Bloku', a part of the capital Tirana, originally reserved exclusively for the political elite. Some wonder whether the dictator is still there, twitchily peering out between the curtains, watching the people spill in and out of the bars and wondering what happened to his great experiment in Utopia.

How others see them

Foreign observers of Albanians can be divided into two categories: those who have never been to Albania, and those who have.

The former know only the negative stories of blood

feuds, prostitution, drugs, violence and general evil. One commentator cynically put it that those in power might be happy with this negative view by outsiders since the fewer foreigners coming to Albania, the stronger their hold on society. The latter, those who venture to Albania, are pleasantly surprised, not least because their expectations are low. They find all the positives that are omitted in the general narrative.

By and large, Albanians are viewed either as victims or as potential criminals. But Lord Byron admired Albanian courage and the anthropologist Edith Durham, a redoubtable British lady who spent much time travelling in the north of Albania at the beginning of the 20th century, developed a great respect for Albanian traditions, notably '*ndera*' – honour, and '*besa*' – trust. She felt that they had not been treated well by the world community. This is a view echoed by many Albanians.

> **66 By and large, Albanians are viewed either as victims or as potential criminals. 99**

Albania's nearest neighbours are not so overwhelming in their affection for Albanians. Some of them lay claim to Albanian territory, and some have observed that their countries host a large influx of Albanian immigrants who, it might be argued, take the jobs of the locals. However, others acknowledge that Albanians are merely doing the jobs that the locals don't want to do.

Meanwhile, the views of foreigners actually living in Albania are often coloured by the differences between their cultures. For example, the Japanese feel uneasy about the lack of collective effort 'for the common good', the Swiss complain of the 'absence of order', and the Germans grumble about the endemic 'breaking of rules'.

What is certain is that Albanians, while welcoming outsiders, have an in-built need to preserve their identity from outside influence. They have managed to do so for centuries and have every intention of continuing to do so in this one.

How they see themselves

The Albanians believe they are the smartest people in the world, and it is the combined effects of history, fate, terrible governments and rapacious neighbours that have conspired to keep them down.

> **The word *'i zgjuar'* (smart) has a particular resonance.**

The word *'i zgjuar'* (smart) has a particular resonance. It is about 'outsmarting' others. It is the ability to get one over on your enemy or anybody who is not your friend or family. It is the ability to reach an objective by the fastest, most convenient means even if it entails excluding an important detail. It is getting in front of somebody at a set of traffic lights. Albanians have a grudging respect for rich, successful people, because they are obviously *'i zgjuar'*. Politicians, whether liked or hated, are admired because they are *'i zgjuar'* and because smart people can survive better than those who slavishly follow the rules and do things the hard way. Naturally, the politicians themselves may have to perpetuate an image of *'i zgjuar'* in order to gain respect from the population.

> **❝ Politicians, whether liked or hated, are admired because they are *'i zgjuar'*. ❞**

For those who have not made it in the rich and successful stakes, it is sufficient to do smart things every now and again, to remind themselves of their cleverness, preferably at the expense of someone else.

North is north and south is south

Guides to Albania are usually prefaced with a note about the country being divided between the Ghegs and Tosks. Albanians are aware of this linguistic description but prefer to divide themselves into 'northerners' and 'southerners' as this carries an emotional significance. It's not quite the same thing, but it's more meaningful.

An English writer once reported that the Ghegs (Northerners) were 'tough, uncouth, aggressive' while the Tosks (Southerners) were 'educated, civilised, Italianate'. This would come as some surprise to the occasional *raki*-sodden old man from the south or the suave, urbane and multi-lingual sophisticate from the north. Indeed the urbane man from the south and the *raki*-sodden man from the north may not recognise the description either.

In the eyes of southern Albanians the northerners are intense, even fanatical; they are hot blooded and sensitive to slights and never far from a gun to defend their honour. Southerners believe blood feuds to be alive and well in the North.

To northern Albanians the southerners are less trustworthy. A northerner claims that if he

❝Southerners are loquacious; northerners are taciturn.❞

makes a promise he will move heaven and earth to honour his word whereas he will accuse a southerner of breaking his word 'if circumstances change'. When it comes to fighting for a cause, the northerners may be picky about when and where to fight and discretion is the better part of valour; the southerners, who are quicker to take arms for a cause, claim this is mere cowardice.

Southerners are loquacious; northerners are taciturn. Some say this is because of the difference in climate and may be the reason why the former tended to gravitate to Italy and Greece and the latter to Northern Europe and Britain. The northerners felt they got the better deal: while they lost the sunny Mediterranean, they gained a global language for their children.

Minorities

Within Albania's borders there are a small number of Serbs, Montenegrins and Macedonians, as well as a larger ethnic Greek population. Relations with these groups tend to reflect the wider national antagonisms between the respective governments, and thorny issues are related to history rather than minority rights.

There are also the Roma who operate on the periphery of society, and are low-key and unaggressive, while 'Egyptians' are more assimilated Roma (or from different stock altogether, according to some). The latter are looked upon by Albanians with less hostility than the former.

> **❝ Unlike the Roma, the Vlachs are fully assimilated and, indeed, many Albanians may not be aware that their friend is Vlach. ❞**

The other major group are the Vlachs or Aromanians who speak a language related to Latin and Romanian and who have lived all over the Balkan region for as long as history can document. Unlike the Roma, the Vlachs are fully assimilated and, indeed, many Albanians may not be aware that their friend is Vlach since the names are not always recognisably Vlach, and Vlachs prefer to keep their identity low profile and their language within the family. On account of how the language sounds to them, Albanians refer to them as 'Lazi Fazis'.

How they see others

Stereotypes abound in the mind of an Albanian.

The Greeks are seen as lazy and proud. They are thought to rely too much on ancient history when claiming their superiority. The Greek economic crisis is viewed with mixed feelings – unhappiness that so many Albanians are unable to find work and therefore remittances home have fallen (a high proportion of Albanians prefer to work in Greece rather than Albania), and a feeling of 'having it coming to them' – rather like watching a proud, swaggering man disappear down a manhole.

Nothing unites the Albanians more than enmity towards the Greeks with whom there are unresolved historical and territorial issues. For example, the Albanian national football

> **66 Nothing unites the Albanians more than enmity towards the Greeks with whom there are unresolved historical and territorial issues. 99**

team which does not exactly excel in international games manages to pull together and defeat the Greek team as if the spirit of the Albanian national hero Skanderbeg has appeared on the football pitch to lead them against their traditional rival.

With the Kosovars there is an ambiguity. There's a logic that speakers of the same language should be part of the same country. The argument goes that it would not only right traditional wrongs and keep the Albanian-speaking family together but, more importantly, it would annoy one of the traditional enemies, the Serbs. However, having Kosovo join Albania would be like having a brother who has lived abroad for a long time coming back to live in the house. You feel duty-bound to have him, but you have developed different likes and dislikes while he's been away and you have different vocabulary and it would be an uncomfortable experience for both. The family ties are strong enough for an

> **66 The family ties are strong enough for an Albanian to be proud when a Kosovar achieves greatness. 99**

Albanian to be proud when a Kosovar achieves greatness ('They're really Albanians, you know') but not strong enough when a Kosovar does something bad ('Of course, they're just Kosovars').

The average Albanian knows little about the Serbs apart from their historical incursions into Albanian territory and the Kosovan crisis*. However, the Serbs are deemed to be the traditional enemy and as such the occasional abusive graffiti about them on the walls in Tirana is only surpassed by those about the Greeks.

The Italians, unlike the Greeks, have no territorial disputes with the Albanians. They are more tolerated, despite negative stories regarding the treatment of Albanian immigrants in Italy. It is true that Italy did

*The fight in 1999 for control of Kosovo between Serbs and ethnic Albanian citizens of Kosovo.

annex Albania as part of the Italian empire; on the other hand, the Italians did construct the nicest boulevards and buildings that still exist in Tirana. What is more, a generation of Albanians have been fed on Italian TV and Italian pasta and pizza. Albanians enjoy showing off their Italian, learnt through the TV. The positives, in fact, outweigh the negatives.

Despite being occupied by the Turks for nearly 500 years, the Albanians do not have the same antagonism towards them as they do towards, for example, the Greeks. Some say this is because during that time they adopted Turkish words, names, the religion, the food, and possibly a byzantine public administration. In short, so runs the argument, 'they don't hate them, because they are like them'.

A special place is reserved in Albanian hearts for the Americans. After World War I Woodrow Wilson backed Albanian independence against other European

> **They adopted Turkish words, names, the religion, the food, and possibly a byzantine public administration.**

nations who sought to divide it up between its neighbours. America, it is believed, was responsible for wresting control of Kosovo from the Serbs; and America continues to send armies of Peace Corps volunteers to various places around Albania, carrying out projects and trying to cultivate good will.

The British are admired for their culture and honesty and, of course, their language without which no

Albanian could hope to emigrate to the UK, Australia, Canada or the US, or get a decent job with a good company in Albania.

Biografi

Biografi is broadly translated as 'self identity' or 'personal history'. Under communism, *biografi e mirë* (good biography) meant the person was a loyal party activist. *Biografi e keqe* (bad biography) was given to those and their family who had fallen out of political favour, had been imprisoned, had been landlords or had fought with the non-communist partisans. Often those with bad *biografi* and their families became 'untouchables'.

> **66 Under communism, 'good biography' meant the person was a loyal party activist. These days it tends to be defined as having money. 99**

These days a good *biografi*, or a good family background, tends to be defined as having money rather than education, and is used especially about those who may ostentatiously sport the trappings of wealth. Often these seem to be mutually exclusive. Just as those with good *biografi* were role models in the past, so they are still in the present, with money replacing good party credentials and, supposedly, making them good husband material for daughters.

Character

In each Albanian there are two Albanians. The inner, true Albanian, is naturally generous, warm-hearted, honest, hard-working and loyal. However, this is locked inside the other Albanian which is the public face. The public face demands that you be ready for any potential threat by exuding aggression, and that you don't volunteer for the public good without being seen to directly benefit yourself, otherwise you will look silly. The fear of other people's judgements reinforces this exterior shell.

Logically, in a different environment, an Albanian may have no need to wear this defensive exterior and the natural disposition

> **66 For an Albanian if a situation is difficult it's because that's the way it is. 99**

shines through. This is why outside their country Albanians belie their own stereotype; foreigners find that Ardiana or Dritan work hard, give of themselves for no return, and volunteer for things to help others as much as is needed. However, when Ardiana or Dritan return to Albania, the public armour is put back on.

It is as it is

Some cultures believe that difficulties exist in order to test their mettle and it is a matter of personal pride to take them as a challenge to overcome: they put their best foot forward and try to be equal to the task. For an Albanian if a situation is difficult it's because that's the way it is (*ashtu eshte*). There is no attempt to mitigate it, change the situation or even try to make sure that it never happens again. No, the preferred – and sensible – option is to adapt oneself to the difficulty.

Trying again is regarded as a pointless exercise because if you failed once, you're bound to fail again. If somebody is watching you, you might go through the motions of trying to do the thing in order to avoid looking like a loser. But this is for show: there is no hope or belief that you will succeed. In fact, the more you try, the more reasons you can think of for not continuing.

Directness

While Albanians are not always ready to tell you what they really think, when it comes to eliciting information from others, they can be unnervingly direct. Some cultures have a filtering process between thought and word which sifts a question in the head to determine whether it passes the test of politeness, diplomacy and possibly ambiguity.

> 66 With Albanians, thought and word lie adjacent with an open connecting door. 99

With Albanians, thought and word lie adjacent with an open connecting door. A foreigner may find it disconcerting to be asked, 'Where are you from?', 'Do you have children?', 'Are you married?', all refreshingly simple and straightforward. Any attempts by the outsider to parry the question with an embarrassed laugh and a vague reply will invite the same question but put more forcefully, as though he or she didn't understand it the first time round.

Similarly, some cultures use all manner of long-winded phrases to ask people to do something. A boss from a less direct culture might say: 'When you have time, can you do the report, please?' (He means, of course, 'Do the report, and do it now.') An Albanian will interpret this request literally as if it was something one might care to do if one wants to. The result is, inevitably, that he doesn't do it because he wasn't able to fit it in between drinking coffee with friends and doing nothing in particular. An Albanian boss just says 'Do it!', circumventing any need for decoding.

Saving face

Albanians rarely show envy or shame. This would be an admission that they are lacking in some way. They may be envious, but they will cleverly turn it round to somehow ascribe blame to the thing they covet or the person who may trigger their jealousy.

If an Albanian manages to get a EU or other non-Albanian passport, enabling him to travel or work abroad without a visa, you don't hear from those around him such comments as 'You lucky thing' or 'I wish I had one'. The Albanian default mode is to criticise the passport holder for his lack of patriotism and pride in being Albanian: in fact, anything to balance out the bad they are feeling at his success.

By the same token, any criticism, no matter how well intended, must be turned around on the critic, and the slightest criticism can be winkled out from an apparently harmless comment. Their natural reaction to a learned discourse is to find fault with what has been said or with the speaker, unless that person has been deemed to have 'superior status', in which case the information is listened to uncritically and with unqualified praise. The 'who' is more important than the 'what'.

> **66 Not losing face is a prime motivator in people's interactions. 99**

Not losing face is a prime motivator in people's interactions. The phrase 'I'm sorry, I don't know' is rarely heard. People will try to bluff their way through the conversation, taking care not to reveal ignorance. The politicians' prime objective when being interviewed on television is not to impart anything particularly meaningful, but to avoid giving the impression they don't know what they're talking about. The problem often is that the more they try to avoid giving this impression the greater the likelihood that they give it.

By the same token, any professor worth his salt, in

order not to compromise the integrity of his profession, will never admit to not knowing something; and an employee will bluster through his answers to a question in order not to give the impression he doesn't know something that he feels he ought to. Self-deprecation is a minority activity.

Good at adapting to change

Albania, to the Albanians, has undergone a head-spinning series of changes since the end of Communism. Society has erupted in an orgy of free market activity and individual rights being asserted – those at the top having more rights. With the mass movement of people who have come down from the villages to the cities, whole ways of life and traditions have been

> **66 When they move outside Albania they rarely stay within their own community, but usually blend in with the existing one. 99**

lost. It is possible in the cities to see old ladies in traditional clothing and men wearing traditional hats reminiscent of the villages they left behind.

The fact that Albanians are arguably more used to change than any other European can be seen in how well they fit into other societies when they move outside Albania. In these countries they rarely stay within their own community, but usually blend in with the existing one.

However, there is one aspect of life that Albanians doggedly cling to. Shops give the price with an extra nought, so that a bottle of water is quoted as costing 500 Lek with the understanding that you will give them 50 Lek. This is a legacy of the currency change in 1965 when one new Lek replaced 10 old Lek. Older British people who remember can smugly point out that their currency was changed overnight in 1971 from 240 pennies to 100 pence in a pound with minimal hitches. The French can, in a similar superior vein, declare that they introduced the new Franc to replace 100 old Francs in 1960 with only about 20 years of confusion. The Albanians are able to rejoin proudly that their multi-tasking skills extend to being able to think in two currency values at once, suggesting that the foreigner is somehow deficient in not being able to do so.

66 Their multi-tasking skills extend to being able to think in two currency values at once. 99

Opinioni

Opinioni, or how others see you, is the force that guides an Albanian's actions. In fact so much weight is placed on what others think of you that your whole life is geared to avoiding yourself or your family being criticised or talked about. As gossiping ranks at the same level as discussing politics in terms of things to do, everybody's worst nightmare is to be its target. To avoid this ignominy, people tend to shun doing anything that makes them stand out or – even worse – makes them the object of ridicule.

One of many concerns for women is to be talked about for not dressing 'well', resulting in careful make-up and a certain degree of sartorial conservatism (unless it's the sort of flashiness that their friends admire).

Opinioni is everywhere. It is in the gym where women do not overdo the exercises lest they break out in a sweat. A steady pace on the cycling machine

> **66 People tend to shun doing anything that makes them stand out or that makes them the object of ridicule. 99**

while keeping in touch with friends on the mobile phone fits the bill much better. Men constantly check themselves in mirrors to make sure they are still presentable. *Opinioni* is the reason that, in the car, the rear view mirror is positioned in such a way as to allow the driver to check his designer stubble, or her hair.

Eccentricity is therefore unacceptable. Of course, there are the artists who appear to cross the boundaries. However, this is within the strict limits of professional permissibility: a pony-tail and 'I don't care about convention' shabby clothes are a mark of the profession, not of the individual's desire to be different or to push cultural limits.

Deviant behaviour is a social faux pas, and everybody is expected to conform to the unwritten mores of doing things the way everybody else does, unless they are clearly a bit bonkers, or foreign. Consequently, it is a society where much time is spent adorning the label, while the contents are neglected. This applies to people and to products. It is why Albanians distrust Albanian products and prefer imported items, for both their prestige and perceived reliability.

Attitudes & Values

Planning

To say that Albanians cannot plan would be a severe simplification of the truth. They would claim that there is no point in planning as things go wrong. Planning is merely a futile attempt by humans to control the environment and destiny. This is impossible as both have a will of their own.

66 Albanians do not plan meetings in advance because other things are sure to come up. 99

Thus, Albanians do not plan meetings in advance because other things are sure to come up. Indeed, it is a mark of friendship to drop all your prior commitments because a good friend has just called and invited you for a coffee. Depending on the level of friendship, you will either accept the invitation, air-brushing all other arrangements, or apologise for not being able to make it if the caller is lower down your personal pecking order. There is none of the Anglo-Saxon thought process: 'What cheek to call me out of the blue and invite me for coffee as though I was doing nothing else!' Northern Europeans view spontaneity with the contempt they feel it deserves, unless it's planned spontaneity. Albanians have lifted spontaneity to the level of a national sport.

Such spontaneity has meant that there is little use for timetables. In the absence of a well-planned public transport system, the country is criss-

66 Albanians have lifted spontaneity to the level of a national sport. 99

crossed with armies of minibuses in various states of disrepair which ply their trade vocally. From a travelling minibus, a driver – or his friend who hangs dangerously from the doorway – will shout 'Durres' or 'Tirana' or whatever town they are bound for to passers-by in the hope that they will abandon whatever they were going to do and just hop on the minibus and go to another town. Indeed, it is only at the insistence of the International Aviation Authorities that airlines flying out of Nënë (Mother) Teresa Airport do not have stewardesses hanging out the door shouting 'Munich!' or 'Gatwick!' to passers-by walking along the tarmac.

The refusal to plan and the consequent surprise at emerging situations have found their way into

Albanian grammar. As well as the universal armoury of indicatives, imperatives and subjunctives that characterise verb forms, there is the 'admirative' mood which is a special verbal construction used to express surprise at the unexpected, a sort of exclamation mark enshrined in a grammatical construction; for instance, 'Oh you've come!' (you did tell me you were coming but I was doing something else at the time, so it didn't register), or 'The post's arrived!' (how did the postman ever find us since we don't actually have an address!).

66 There is a special verbal construction used to express surprise at the unexpected. 99

It would be nice to think that a perfect system of improvisation could be substituted for lack of planning. But this is not the case. An unforeseen event, particularly a crisis, is characterised by a short period of questioning as to why it happened and then an attempt to mitigate the more serious consequences of the event while simultaneously trying to blame other people. This is followed shortly afterwards by a repeat of the same unforeseen event and a duplication of the blame process, all of which is accompanied by plenty of verbal 'admirative' moods.

Religion

It is said that Albania is 70% Muslim, 20% Orthodox and 10% Catholic. In fact, real figures vary and the number of Muslims is also said to be as low as 40%, but all this is probably of greater interest to outsiders than to Albanians. The Albanian poet Pashko Vaso proclaimed in the 19th century that the religion of Albanians was 'Albanianism'. His relegation of religion to the back seat was, and still is, a general reflection of how most people actually feel.

> **66 The Albanian poet Pashko Vaso proclaimed that the religion of Albanians was 'Albanianism'. 99**

Religion is a nominal label which merely defines the Albanians' background in the same way as the French may call themselves 'Catholics' or the English 'Anglicans'. They are 'tribal labels' which are not really relevant in day-to-day life except when a Christian and Muslim wish to get married, though generally there is no problem there either. Religious tolerance takes precedence over religious practice. Thus, a Muslim confided that she preferred going with her friends to the Catholic church because 'they do a good service, especially at Christmas, although the Orthodox do a nicer Easter'. Muslims and Christians alike go on pilgrimages to the Church of Saint Anthony ('Shna Andout') to cure illnesses, for females to find a husband, and everybody to pray for miracles in general. The visit of the Pope to Tirana in 2014 was attended en masse by Albanians of all creeds. Similarly, Western surprise at 'Muslims sheltering Jews' during World War II is greeted with some bemusement by

Albanians who do not quite see the contradiction that the rest of the world apparently does.

Religious extremism and public practice are rare, although there are attempts by outsiders to whip up religious fundamentalism. Certainly, spotting a woman wearing a burka in Albania is almost as rare as seeing a nun in Riyadh. However, by the same token, Albania plays host to many religions including the Bektashis, a branch of Shia Islam whose practices differ from other branches of Islam and which is tolerant of other religions. They have their world headquarters in Albania, having been expelled from Turkey in 1925. There are also numerous Protestant churches and missionaries who are attracted to the fact that Albania is Muslim enough to warrant attempts at conversion on the one hand, but liberal enough to allow missionaries to be in the country on the other. A number of Albanians go to the Christian Evangelical churches run by Americans and other nationalities, some to try a new faith and some simply to practise their English.

> **❝ Spotting a woman wearing a burka in Albania is almost as rare as seeing a nun in Riyadh. ❞**

It was Enver Hoxha who tried to abolish all religions. Although the Turks had some success in reducing Christian worship in favour of Islam either by tax incentives or at the point of a sword, in 1967 Hoxha declared Albania to be the 'first atheist country' by

24

destroying churches and mosques and imprisoning and killing priests and imams along with banning private religious observance under threat of jail or death. After the demise of communism, people flocked back to the church either out of religious conviction or because it was the thing to do, like visiting relatives. It's a great opportunity to catch up with friends, and the chats after the service may be as long as the service itself.

Processes

In some cultures, following processes and procedures is revered as the proper way to achieve one's objective: setting a goal and clearly defining each step to reach it. The focus is on completing each step before going on to the next one.

> **66 At all times Albanians will focus on achieving the end result as quickly as possible. 99**

Albanians will pooh-pooh this way of doing things. At all times they will focus on achieving the end result as quickly as possible. Admittedly some corners will be cut, things missed out, issues glossed over, but in the end the objective is reached, however imperfectly. In short, getting to the end as fast as possible justifies the means. Moreover, a person gains points of honour in deliberately doing it differently and somehow cheating the gods or the rules.

Getting a driving licence is a good example. One might think that the licence is evidence that a person has gone through the process of learning to drive and is therefore sufficiently qualified to be in charge of a vehicle on a public highway. If you are Albanian it is a merely a permit to show the police. Obtaining the document in the quickest way possible may mean coming to an agreement with the driving test examiner. By doing this, you will get admiration from your peers for defeating the ponderous system of paying money to take lots of lessons, while avoiding the embarrassment of being seen in the streets as a learner driver and the ignominy of ultimately being failed.

> **❝ No matter that there are no steps to the front door or that there are live wires sticking out of the wall... it is built. ❞**

Another example is the newly-constructed house. No matter that there are no steps to the front door, only a 'temporary' wooden plank, or that there are live wires sticking out of the wall ('Just make sure you don't touch them or it'll serve you right if you get electrocuted'), it is built.

Similarly, a student might spend many nights on the Internet trying to find a ready-made answer for his assignment. The fact that it might have been quicker to think through and answer the question without help points to three significant features of the Albanian psyche. Firstly, the focus is on getting it done, even if illegally or wrongly. Secondly, the emphasis is on the action itself rather than why it is being done (in this case to educate and learn rather than merely to complete a task). Thirdly, it is the Albanians' instinct to do the task in a different way from what is suggested, thereby showing how smart they are.

Discussions

Discussions also fall victim to this phenomenon. The object of a discussion in many parts of the world is to exchange ideas in the belief that in the process new ideas will emerge and thus add value to the dialogue. For Albanians, the object of a discussion is to show the other person that your point of view is right, not by clever argument or logical refutation of the other person's argument but by overt acts of aggression to demonstrate the consequences of being disagreed with.

> **66 For Albanians, the object of a discussion is to show the other person that your point of view is right. 99**

Not surprisingly, therefore, very little is ever achieved in such exchanges. Political debate is often a matter of who can shout the loudest or who can make the most effective threats in the belief that this is democracy in action (as opposed to totalitarianism, where you are not allowed to say anything).

The process of elimination

Another procedure that Albanians often avoid is the process of elimination. If a machine (or a human being, for that matter) is not functioning, some nationalities will try to isolate the problem by eliminating the unlikely causes, step by step. Albanians consider this method to be rather tedious and think it might be better to take a wild guess and try to fix what you think is wrong. Indeed, professionals feel they have a licence to make wild guesses. In medicine, it may happen that a person is given the wrong pills because the doctor has not bothered to examine the patient but has made an on-the-spot diagnosis on the basis of a given description of the symptoms.

Hospitality

Albanians rank amongst the most hospitable people in Europe, but mainly towards family, close friends and foreigners. The phrase 'God in the House, Guest in the House' is true for many countries, but is perhaps why Albanians don't invite others to their house very often. Having God in the house is a big responsibility and the house is probably not worthy of God. There is a danger (it is argued) that the guest might feel let down and, worse still, tell everybody how unworthy the house was. Those who are invited to someone's home should therefore realise it is not only a gesture of hospitality, it is a mark of the trust placed in you that you won't judge them or gossip about them. It's an honour bestowed on the few.

Custom dictated that guests were under the protection of the host who was expected to treat them royally, protect them while they were under his roof and take direct responsibility should any misfortune befall them. This was true even if they were sworn enemies. It was honouring the tradition not the person.

> **66 Those who are invited to someone's home should realise it is a mark of the trust placed in you that you won't judge them or gossip about them. 99**

The foreigner is like God and is treated as such. Albanians will be delighted that the foreigner has come from their rich country (all foreigners are rich) and will treat him or her with courtesy if they respond in kind.

It is therefore understandable why Albanians sheltered Albanian and foreign Jews during World War II. It was the time-honoured obligation of hospitality, irrespective of religion. This overrode any other consideration. As in other occupied countries, the Nazis threatened those who sheltered Jews that they could expect severe retribution, summary execution or being sent to a concentration camp. The cost to benefit calculation in the German mind didn't exist in Albania. In fact, it had the opposite effect. The raising of the stakes heightened the Albanian sense of honour because of the increase in risk to life and limb.

This was not a matter of a brave few but the mental attitude of a whole country. While the same logic can result in less positive consequences in modern day Albania, for example, overtaking a car on a hairpin bend on the side of a mountain or cycling against the busy traffic on a fast road, it did mean that at the time no Jewish refugee was killed by the Nazis in Albania.

Similarly, during World War II, when parts of the Italian army occupying Albania decided they didn't want to fight any more, the Albanians took them in, with many working on farms as labourers despite the risk to their hosts of summary execution. Again, this emboldened their sense of honour. An Albanian who sheltered four Italians in the barn could legitimately lord it over his neighbour who sheltered only three. Even the traditional enemy, the Greeks, when fleeing from their civil war after World War II, were given shelter along with their cattle, and all returned intact to Greece when it was safe to do so. During the Kosovo crisis, Albanians opened their doors to their ethnic brothers and whole families were sardined into their small flats. Respect for the custom continues to this day.

The Albanian code of hospitality extends to other

> **66 The Albanian code of hospitality extends to other Albanians. It is a matter of honour to insist on paying for your counterpart's drink. 99**

parts of life and to other Albanians. It is a matter of honour to insist on paying for your counterpart's drink. Thus, if you see two people arguing in a bar in other countries, the argument is often about politics, while some may grab each other's lapels in the wake of an excess of alcohol. In Albania, the near-violent squabble is about each party's insistence on paying the bill.

Shok and Mik

Although both *Shok* and *Mik* are translated into English as 'friend', there is a distinction. A *Shok* is a friend acquired along the journey of life, while your *Mik* is closer, someone who is either related to the family or is treated as part of the family, so is welcome to drop in on you at any time without having arranged it.

As an Englishman's home is his castle, the castle in Albania is not the physical building but the concept of the family and those close to it, and the *Mik* is part of that circle. Once accepted into it, there are accompanying obligations. These might be a request to bend the rules to accede to some request or favour if it is in the *Mik*'s power to do so.

> **❝ Your *Mik* is someone who is either related to the family or is treated as part of the family, so is welcome to drop in on you at any time. ❞**

The *Shok* has also played a specific role in Albanian society. In a country where everybody is wary of strangers, often the only way to get to know new people is through having a mutual friend or an endorsement by way of a named introduction. And since news of bad behaviour can travel through the friendship grapevine (*Mikseria* or *Shoqeria*), and render you persona non grata in your immediate circle, *Shok* also minimises anti-social behaviour.

To the younger generation, the distinction between *Shok* and *Mik* is not entirely clear.

The Family

The family is the beginning and the end of the reason for an Albanian's existence. The concept of family includes not just the immediate relatives but also the grandparents, the uncles and aunts, the cousins and beyond – the '*fis*' or the clan, and the wider extended family.

> **66 The family is the beginning and the end of the reason for an Albanian's existence. 99**

The family used to play an important role in deciding what job a person was going to do, who they were going to marry and how to avoid bringing shame on the family. Brothers had the role of being their sister's protectors, and the brother's opinion could be as influential as the parents'.

When the tradition of arranged marriages began to

decline, it was important to find out where a potential mate was from in order to prevent marriage between distant cousins, especially on the male side. This is still the case in villages. However, as people have gravitated towards the towns, such rules are less in evidence and families are becoming more nuclear. The elderly complain that their grandchildren seem to owe a greater loyalty to their friends than to their family.

Because of the cost of housing and the emphasis on the extended family, there are often three generations under one roof. The youngest son is expected to look after the parents when they are too old to look after themselves, and he may live with his parents when he gets married. This is a source of tension between daughter-in-law and mother-in-law, with the husband caught in the middle owing loyalty to his mother who tries to maintain the mother-son bond and to his wife who is expected to accept this.

66 There are often three generations under one roof. 99

While both parents are at work, grandparents play a role in the children's upbringing, often spoiling them rotten because it is easier to give in than to lay down the law, and they know they will not have to cope with the longer-term consequences.

The idea of putting an elderly relative in an old people's home is shocking to the Albanians. The elderly are still greatly respected and cared for in a way that the elderly of other nations would love to be.

The children

Albanians lavish physical affection on children, both their own and other people's, hugging them and pinching their cheeks. Babies are swaddled in many layers of protective clothes as though being equipped for a Siberian winter and children's school bags are carried for them by parents or grandparents. The smothering and protection may continue to adulthood, reinforcing the mutual dependency that is so important in an Albanian family. Furthermore, if parents are not thought to be displaying proper parenting skills, such as letting a child run wild or taking it out without the mandatory layers of clothing, they will feel free to tell them so, even if they are total strangers.

The role of men and women

There is an unspoken law about Albanian womanhood. Women are born to serve their brothers, to cook for them and act as mother when their mother is not there. They dress as nicely as possible to attract a male and, once married, they lavish the same attention on their husbands as they did on their brothers. They allow the men to act as though they are in control, letting them use masculine body language with great gusto and speak in a masculine way, and they put up with the men's enthusing over the trappings of manhood – the car and football and talk of manly pursuits.

They pay great deference to all this; they fawn and
simper and bat their eyelashes in a subservient manner, whilst doing all the work in the home and outside
it. As the poet Andon Cajupi put it:

What about your husband
Lounging by the fountain?
Oh, my wretched woman,
You run, too, the household!

However, all is not what it seems. Women manipu-
late the upbringing of their sons in an artful way. The
sons are brought up to have everything done by the
women: shopping, cooking, housework, clothes-
buying, and decisions on education. This means that
their mothers – and then their wives – have made
them unable to function without a female. It has been
known for a wife to put stick-on notes with the days
of the week on various clothes to tell her husband
which clothes to wear when she goes away.

Reverse dependency does not apply, although the
women are successful in making the men feel indispensable, at least at the beginning of marriage. As
time goes on the men get cut out from life because of
their limited survival skills (for example, being unable
even to turn an egg from a spherical object into something edible). The house becomes alien territory and in
old age all the men can do is play chess and dominoes
in the park or any available green space with all the

other old men who have been made superfluous. The shift in power is also reflected in physique, as the old men shrink while the women expand.

> **66 The shift in power is also reflected in physique, as the old men shrink while the women expand. 99**

Conflict, however, is not far away as the consensus between generations is breaking down. Having made her son totally dependent on a woman, the mother-in-law fears that her son's wife will encourage him to do things for himself. Many a fight begins with the mother-in-law saying such things as 'You are letting my son iron his own clothes! What sort of wife are you?'

As women increasingly rebel against their traditional role and men begin to enjoy cooking and relating to their children in a meaningful way, at least in urban areas, the family structure is beginning to change.

Obsessions

Tidiness

It is no exaggeration to say that Albanians are tremendously house-proud. A substantial part of the household expenses goes towards cleaning agents, sprays, brushes, wipes and the like. If money is not available, the thrifty housewife will turn to ingenious ways of keeping the place clean, taking as much time as is necessary to create a spotless home. Visitors, who are required to take their shoes off when entering the abode, are immediately aware that everything has its place and woe betide anybody who messes it up.

The inside is not what the decayed, damp and often crumbling exterior would suggest. If there is a balance between external and internal, it would be that there is so much focus on the inside that the outside is ignored and left to others to take care of.

There is reluctance on the part of Albanians to indulge in community actions such as tidying the environment or creating grass-roots initiatives to mend public property and look after public green spaces (which are a magnet for property developers with good connections). The indifference of successive governments to involve themselves in public projects – either out of lack of desire or lack of ability – leaves a yawning chasm of nothing being done.

66 'Outside' is someone else's responsibility and the care of it is left to fate or to Mother Nature. 99

The resultant detritus is probably the first thing that visitors to Albania notice. In the streets, the bins are overflowing. Young and old carelessly discard papers, throwing them on the ground or out of the car window. 'Outside' is someone else's responsibility and the care of it is left to fate or to Mother Nature, who appears to have her hands full. In Albania, she is used to that and may have even given up.

Mobile phones

The mobile phone could have been invented especially for a society that does not plan. In Albania, it is used primarily to bridge the planning gap – a way of papering over the unexpected in order to cause minimal disruption. It is also a status symbol. A businessman sits down to a meeting or to a meal in a restaurant and lays three or more mobile phones on the table, rather like a millionaire sits at a casino table and spreads out his chips. The signal is 'I'm so important I need all these phones to handle all the calls I get.' The real reason is that each one carries a different network provider SIM card to take advantage of the various price incentives that are offered from time to time.

> **66 In Albania, the mobile is used primarily to bridge the planning gap – a way of papering over the unexpected. 99**

Superstitions

Most urban Albanians pride themselves on their lack of superstition which they think of as the mark of villagers and uneducated people. No educated urban Albanian would accept, or admit to, the practice of mixing ram's blood into the foundations of a new building for good luck as they might still do in the countryside.

However, it is OK to consult the horoscope to see

what the future holds, just to make sure. It is better to hang a stuffed toy, a horseshoe, garlic or countless other artefacts from your apartment building to deflect the evil eye, just in case such a thing as an evil eye exists.

If your hands are warm, there will be a sneaking suspicion that you are not being honest. And just remember when you take off your shoes to make sure they are pointing in the same direction; don't pour water into a glass that already has some water in it; and if you spill salt, spill some sugar too. It's better to be safe than sorry and only sensible to take precautions. It's not being superstitious, it's just being careful.

> **❝ Don't pour water into a glass that already has some water in it; and if you spill salt, spill some sugar too. ❞**

What Albanian grandmother would not admit to being able to read the future from the coffee grounds at the bottom of a cup? Not only does it elevate her to mythical status in the family but it can also give her the opportunity to decide someone's fate: by 'reading' it, it has to be true...

Going abroad

It is a dream of many Albanians to visit and to work in London. It is not uncommon for those who have never been to London to say, 'I love London.' This is because for most it is the impossible dream. (Actually, the real dream is going to America, but in terms of difficulty, distance and expense, this is like trying to get to Mars as opposed to flying to the Moon.)

Albanians who have lived in the UK and worked incredibly long hours to keep themselves fed (and often feeding their relatives in Albania) cannot do themselves the dishonour of telling those at home how difficult it really was. They talk it up to show others what a wonderful decision it was to live in the UK and especially London. Even so, many would still prefer to work hard in the UK than live in Albania.

They will save up and buy a nice car with British number plates to sum up the trappings and the status of one who has lived in London. On returning to live in Albania, it is a sad day indeed when they are eventually forced to exchange the number plate for an Albanian one. There is still some sort of lingering status from having a right-hand drive car, though this may become more of a handicap than an advantage, especially when overtaking, or when presenting documents at the border to the chap in the passport booth. However, it's useful to be able to stop and chat with friends who are walking along the pavement.

> **66** Albanians who have lived in the UK and worked incredibly long hours cannot do themselves the dishonour of telling those at home how difficult it really was. **99**

Leisure & Pleasure

Busy doing nothing

The default setting for a north European is work, and leisure therefore has to be justified; for the Albanians it is the other way round, in that the onus is on justifying work or any other activity that doesn't involve sitting drinking coffee, being with the family or staring vacuously into space. In between trying to get to the

> **❝ The onus is on justifying work or any other activity that doesn't involve sitting drinking coffee ...or staring vacuously into space. ❞**

head of the queue, or being the first to drive off as the traffic lights turn green, there is a lot of inactivity. In fact, if you are seen running in the street it will be assumed you've stolen something.

Albanian men stand around doing nothing in particular. (Doing this in the UK gave rise to their having a bad reputation as they were thought to be up to no good – loitering with intent – as opposed to up to nothing in particular which was the real reason, but a concept that is absent in Britain.)

Whereas Albanian men can stand at street corners for hours, women do not. Women always appear to be going somewhere and walk with a sense of purpose – to pick the child up from the grandparents, to go shopping, to go home and cook, and so on. Paradoxically, in the car the roles are reversed.

41

Women, generally assuming the role of technophobes, drive tentatively, while men drive with exaggerated purpose, losing patience with anybody who gets in their way.

Cafés and coffee

The comfortable alternative to standing around in the street is to sit in a café for hours over one coffee talking animatedly, or simply... sitting. In Albania sitting doing nothing is a natural option due to lack of credible alternatives. In fact, if Albanian life could be divided into theoretical units of sitting in a coffee bar, then life or success could be measured in such units. So, whereas a foreigner might ask himself at the end of the day 'What did I achieve today?', an Albanian might assess his day in terms of how much theoretical

> **66 An Albanian might assess his day in terms of how much theoretical 'coffee time' he had. 99**

'coffee time' he had. This is a measure for other activities; for example, 'It's not a good job because it deprives me of X units of coffee time.' 'It was a good weekend because I had Y units of coffee time.' The cities of Albania are peppered with cafés where men can sit and loiter without intent. In the countryside where cafés are less numerous men have no choice but to stand and stare. The coffee-drinking units also explain why an employee may refuse to work overtime. Though this could mean earning more money, it eats into the sacrosanct leisure time – a privilege from birth.

Drinking coffee has an important role on many levels. For some, the coffee bar is the first place to go after leaving home in the morning and the last place to go before returning home at night. It offers an alternative to home, especially for men, and is the venue for romantic assignations.

Albanians prefer to do business and sign contracts in the neutral territory of a coffee bar. Appearances can be deceptive: those two nice old men chatting over coffee could actually be concluding a million dollar deal, or dreaming of how they might have done if fate hadn't conspired against them.

The *Xhiro*

Between the hours of six and eight in the evening Albanians go out for an evening walk – the *Xhiro*. For many it is a chance to meet and catch up on the gossip with people they would otherwise never see, or for a young woman, decked out in her finery, to try and catch the eye of a particular young man.

The *Xhiro* was popular in communist times when TV was less than compelling and there was nothing else to do. The communist authorities encouraged it because in the open they could keep an eye on what people were doing.

Although the practice is dying out in larger cities as TV and computers offer stronger distractions, it still takes place in smaller towns. In Berat, for example, the *Xhiro* consists of two lines: one of people going up the long street and the other of people coming back, observing a greater discipline as pedestrians than they would do as drivers. Thus, if the boy didn't notice the girl's positive body language the first time round, the girl has a second or even third chance to catch his eye.

Holidays

There are several types of Albanian holiday-makers: those who prefer the beach, those who prefer the mountains and lakes, those who go abroad and those who stay at home. Most prefer the sea. (Kosovars and Macedonian Albanians also head for the Albanian coast as they are from landlocked countries.)

The beaches range from the virgin, where you need a four-wheel-drive car or the pioneer spirit of Lord Byron to help you to get there, to the once virgin beaches which have been transformed into concrete jungles by regulated, unregulated and semi-regulated building. Albanian holiday-makers flock to the unspoilt seaside in increasing numbers, oblivious to the fact that they are spoiling the very thing that attracts them. Indeed, many take great delight in leaving evidence of their stay in the form of discarded items – on the beach, in the street, and in the hotel.

Those who go abroad on holiday consider themselves the privileged few. There is the elite who go shopping in Milan, and their less wealthy counterparts who go to Milan and come back with (empty) carrier bags bearing the name of Milan shops to show off to their friends.

Public holidays

All the major religious festivals – Christmas, Easter and the end of Ramadan – are public holidays. In addition, there are national holidays which include an Independence Day followed by the Day of Liberation. Since the two main political parties cannot agree on whether the 28th or the 29th November is Independence Day, both days are celebrated, but the parties celebrate on different days. To further

> **"Since the two main political parties cannot agree on whether the 28th or the 29th November is Independence Day, both days are celebrated. "**

complicate the basically uncomplicated, the authorities decree that should any holiday fall at a weekend, private companies can decide for themselves whether or not to take the Monday of the following week off.

New Year is a major holiday when families celebrate together and fireworks are let off in the streets.

Gambling

There is a large number of betting cafés and gambling
establishments. The fact that there are so many is partly due to the idea that people expect to get rich rapidly
by setting up such establishments. The same 'get rich
quick' idea is in the minds of those who use them, and
many a family budget has been frittered away in the
hope of winning 'the big one'. Of course, if no win is
forthcoming, it could be because of the black cat in the
street...

Behaviour

Problem solving

Albanians have no time for the tortuous processes of
thinking through problems and solutions that some
cultures indulge in. In fact the first hurdle for an
Albanian is to admit to himself that there is a problem,
especially as this may suggest that the problem was
caused by some mistake or miscalculation on his part.
However, this can easily be overcome if the blame can
be ascribed to others or to forces 'outside his control'.
The former is preferable to the latter.

The second hurdle is admitting to others, especially
outsiders, that there is a problem at all. Albanians will
go to enormous lengths to avoid revealing that there is
anything wrong. In fact, focusing on ways of hiding
the problem or creating excuses may be more impor-

tant than addressing the problem – the 'who' being more important than the 'what'.

In the workplace this covering up can result in the problem being compounded and multiplying, but that is a long-term consequence and what is more important is that covering up deflects the shorter-term blame. Besides, if the problem is not highlighted, it might go away as, God willing, it occasionally does.

You may only be aware that there is a problem when a person actually says 'No problem'. This is when you really need to worry as it means 'There is a problem but I don't want you to know about it, because you might kick up a fuss and make me feel bad.' If it is finally admitted that there is a problem, it is safer to think

> **66 When a person actually says 'No problem', this is when you really need to worry. 99**

up as many reasons as possible why it shouldn't be tackled. In the end this is much more satisfying than finding that one elusive reason why someone should go to the effort of trying to solve it.

Multi-tasking

Few other nations have cultivated multi-tasking to as fine an art as have the Albanians. If Albanian car drivers have a talent for anything (apart from avoiding serious accidents when behind the wheel), it is the ability to drink coffee, smoke a cigarette, speak on the mobile, chat to the person next to them with waving arms, gesticulate angrily at other drivers, press the horn, compose a text message and still have enough arms to drive.

It is not an uncommon sight for a man, his wife and his two children to ride together on a moped. While the man is controlling it, he may be holding an umbrella to protect his family from the rain, and the rest of the family are individually engaged in talking on the phone, checking Facebook, holding animated conversations with lots of arm-waving, and saving each other from falling off.

Even certain TV news stations multi-task by show ing lots of items on one screen as if it is a website. The main picture is in the middle with either the news (and a one-line summary underneath) or interviews or advertisements for potions to eliminate unsightly marks on the body. A banner at the top of the screen announces the date, time and temperature, and at the bot-

> **66 Certain TV news stations show lots of items on one screen as if it is a website. 99**

tom a news ticker displays the headlines in a curious form of English. There may also be a public service announcement and, elsewhere on the screen, another headline and an ad with seizure-inducing flashes. People are quite happy to dart from one section to another, semi-digesting the contents before the screen changes after a few seconds to show new items.

At university, the average classroom has students listening to the lecturer, talking to the person sitting next to them, sending texts, filling in the 'o's in the textbook and looking out of the window – all at the same time. The lecturer is not happy with this because he is restricted to a single activity, which is teaching.

An Albanian feels naked when doing only one task at a time. He has a nagging feeling that he should be doing at least two other things concurrently. When you think you have an Albanian's full attention, be aware that he's probably also deciding what he's going to do at the weekend, judging your dress sense and looking at the person behind you. Don't worry, he's still listening to you in a general sort of way.

> 66 An Albanian feels naked when doing only one task at a time. 99

The car

In the eyes of many Albanian men – and some women, the car holds a special place. It is not just a means of transporting people from A to B: it is a symbol of success and personal prowess and virility. A family may boast of their son to a prospective bride that 'he has a Mercedes' as the last word in desirability. A man may cut back on less essential items such as food, clothes and home repairs in order to be able to sport the ultimate symbol of having made it in life.

Many a driver rejects the wearing of seatbelts as being unmanly. It is not unknown for a passenger to be asked not to buckle up (which would imply a lack of trust), at least in town (where people are watching), though it is more acceptable to wear the strap in the countryside (where there are no prying eyes).

Indicators are considered superfluous, rather like a speedometer or second gear. After all, as a driver put it, 'Why do I need to indicate when I'm pulling out or when I turn? I know where I'm going – why does anybody else need to know?'

The underuse of indicators is more than compensated for by the overuse of the horn. To an outsider, the hooting of the horn is a meaningless noise. To the initiated, just like a mother recognises the different cries of her baby, an Albanian can understand the different noises: the *'the lights turned green two milliseconds ago'* beep to the car in front, or the *'I've been waiting in this queue for the traffic lights for longer than one minute'* beep, or the common *'if you beep at me for something you think I've done wrong, I'll beep back at you just to have the last word'*. The incessant, angry-sounding, single beep is the familiar *'you've double-parked your car and blocked mine. Wherever you are, come back and let me out'*, and the two short staccato beeps is a *'hello'* to a friend in the street.

> **66 The underuse of indicators is more than compensated for by the overuse of the horn. 99**

Finding your way

Under communism, maps and street plans in the hands of anybody but the military were a rare sight. Nowadays, street plans are largely redundant as street names are hardly used and most people are unaware of the names of any streets, including, often, the street where they live. The reason given is that many streets have undergone a change of name from Communist heroes to other types of heroes. Unregulated building means that it is not always clear which street an apartment block is built on, or even whether the relevant department in the town council actually thought of designating a street when the building licence was slipped through.

A typical set of directions to a visitor would be: 'Carry on until you get to the traffic lights and then turn right until you get to where the supermarket was, turn left and walk as far as the sweet factory which was demolished last year and then a bit further until you reach the furniture shop which changed hands five years ago and is now something else, but I can't remember what.'

> **66 Street names are hardly used and most people are unaware of the names of any streets, including, often, the street where they live. 99**

The miracle is that Albanians eventually manage to find the place. It may have to do with having a homing pigeon instinct which outsiders lack. Or it may be to do with perspective. Whereas most westerners, brought up to look at maps and street plans, always imagine directions from a bird's eye view, looking down, Albanians see streets from a horizontal view. Which means that landmarks, not street names, are important, and directions are related in sequence.

Knowledge is power

A foreigner is often struck by how much he or she knows about things, people and situations in Albania and how little it appears that Albanians know about them. This is a misapprehension. Albanians listen to foreigners, not because they are imparting information of which the listener is unaware, but because they want to know exactly how much the outsider knows and measure it against what they know. In this respect, the Albanian may feign naivety or surprise in order to elicit yet more information.

> 66 For Albanians, knowledge is a commodity and therefore power. It is not given away lightly. 99

For Albanians, knowledge is a commodity and therefore power. It is not given away lightly. Even a professor, who is paid to impart knowledge, will always make the students aware that there is some knowledge that he has that they will not be party to, something he is holding back, because if he gives it all away, he has lost all his power.

In an organisation, information is shared on a 'need to know' basis, or rather, on what the information-giver thinks you need to know, which is very little. A Westerner's protestation that an organisation fails because the members have not shared information, and rarely fails because its members know too much, falls on deaf ears. The success of the company is secondary to personal survival and the amount of exclusive information you have. It is believed to be better to be an important, knowledgeable fish in a stagnant pond than a small fish in a thriving one.

Some claim that this is a legacy of communist times when there was a pervasive network of spies and informers so people became naturally tight-lipped, fearing that showing you knew too much was not good for your health.

Eating & Drinking

Food

Albania is rich in dishes with the influence of Turkish, Greek, Italian and Slav cuisines, and in spite of the scarcities of the communist years which elevated bread to a nourishing meal, the country boasts a huge array of traditional dishes, with slightly different emphasis between north, centre and south and between coastal, plain and mountain regions.

Albanians generally eschew ready-cooked meals and prefer to buy the raw ingredients and do the cooking themselves. Frozen food and dry food are rare and probably only bought by foreigners and seriously upwardly-mobile Albanians.

An Albanian will point to two dishes as examples of the national food: *byrek* and *baklava*. *Byrek* is made from layers of pastry filled with meat, tomato and cheese, or cheese and spinach (or nettles in more traditional households). *Byrek*-making is a fine art, and it is the proud boast of an accomplished housewife that she can make *byrek* that knocks the socks off anybody else's.

> 66 A good *baklava* is the mark of a good cook. As one man put it, 'If a wife can do that, she can be forgiven for a lot of shortcomings.' 99

Baklava is also composed of thin layers of pastry, but these are steeped in sugary water and nuts and are an ideal finish to a meal. A good *baklava* is difficult to make and therefore the mark of a good cook. As with *byrek*, the crucial point is the pastry. One man put it, 'If a wife can do that, she can be forgiven for a lot of shortcomings in other areas.'

As a traditional breakfast, many Albanians cannot resist *paça*, a soup made with boiled sheep's head flavoured with herbs and garlic, served with rice. It is perhaps one of those tasty dishes that non-Albanians should eat first and ask questions about afterwards.

When guests are invited for a meal no expense is spared, and they will be encouraged to eat to the point where they will wonder whether they'll ever want to eat again. One of the worst insults for a host is that the guests leave the table feeling even slightly peckish. To ensure this doesn't happen, enough food is prepared for the guest and two imaginary friends.

Alcohol

The king of Albanian drinks is *raki*, a spirit made from grapes or from fruits that are in season. It is the drink of weddings, it is the drink of choice for old men, and it is the drink that is offered to you when you visit someone. You do not refuse unless you want to cause a frisson of unpleasantness, and proclaiming any sort

> **❝ The boast of a true Albanian is that he can tell a good *raki* from a bad one – although nobody will admit that there is such a thing. ❞**

of illness will elicit the reply, 'Then drink this, it'll do you good', and will encourage your host to make you better by plying you with yet more.

The boast of a true Albanian is that he can tell a good *raki* from a bad one – although nobody will admit that there is such a thing.

Raki with well-known labels is available in the shops, but the preferred type is the one available in a plastic cola bottle or, for the more pretentious, in a glass bottle which once contained a 'more inferior' international brand of spirit. This *raki* has been brought in from the countryside, from the countless relatives that may farm no other agricultural product except the fruit needed to make it. A bottle of this will be squirreled away for 'emergencies'.

In towns, foreign spirits are becoming more and more popular, to the extent that no up-and-coming young person worth his salt would ever order a *raki* in a bar; only an international brand of spirits will do. Beer is catching up fast, and in the trendy bars of downtown Tirana it is generally foreign beers that are available to cater to the fashionable younger generation of Albanians.

> 66 It is rare to see a drunk person in the street in Albania. Drinking to excess in public is a shameful act. 99

It is rare to see a drunk person in the street in Albania. As Edith Durham, put it: 'It is the characteristic of a Balkan man... that he can enjoy himself thoroughly and whole-heartedly without ever becoming rowdy or losing his self-respect.'

Drinking to excess in public is a shameful act, and those who indulge will find it difficult to look their fellow man or woman in the eye the next day. Drunkenness is confined to the hallowed surrounds of a wedding or, at times, a small bar where a group of elderly men will argue inanely over glasses of *raki* before shuffling home quietly to sleep it off.

Health & Hygiene

Doctors and medicines used to be as rare in Albania as hen's teeth. During communist times, when medical care was free but often difficult to get other than at a basic level, people tended to treat themselves or rely on old ladies who had generations of knowledge of how to deal with various ailments, using mystical – sometimes smelly – concoctions of things like fish bones and herbs or chopped onions with sugar as a pain-killer, and boiled cherry stalks for kidney complaints. The book that summed up a lot of folk wisdom was *Mjek i Vet Vetes*

> **❝ The book that summed up a lot of folk wisdom, 'Cure yourself', was often one of only two books in the house. ❞**

('Cure yourself') which was often one of only two books in the house. As the ingredients were readily found in the countryside, it was indispensable. (The other book was a copy of the works of Enver Hoxha which was less widely consulted except when a photograph containing a politician who had fallen from favour had to be torn out – just in case a visitor happened to notice it was still there and reported it to the authorities.)

Albanians prefer to avoid doctors and the medical profession unless it is absolutely necessary. The adage 'prevention is better than cure' has no currency, as (it is argued) there are so many illnesses that can be prevented, you would spend all your life just trying to take things to stop them, while the one illness that finally attacks you is the one you didn't expect. Besides, the illness is often blamed on the weather – for which there is no known cure. But if there are any nagging illnesses around, everyone becomes a doctor and suggests a cure that does not involve a visit to the doctor or pharmacy.

Apart from a fundamental distrust of doctors, there is also a culture – particularly among men – of showing how much pain you are in and then demonstrating toughness by putting up with the pain and not resorting to the wimpish taking of painkillers (though these are beginning to creep in as a staple in the home, introduced by the more pragmatic females).

66 If there are any nagging illnesses around, everyone becomes a doctor and suggests a cure. 99

The public not only distrust doctors, they distrust medicine on the grounds that cheap, ineffective generic drugs find their way to Albania. As a result, bathroom cabinets are empty of medicines but often contain bathroom cleaning agents (the bathroom is a place for cleaning yourself, not curing yourself). Thus though pharmacies are plentiful, they generally lack customers.

There are two parallel health care systems. There is the private medical service where you pay at the desk and get a receipt, and the state medical service where you often pay the doctor and nurse directly (without a middle man) and you don't get a receipt.

Dental care

Despite a proliferation of dental practices, dentistry is not widely subscribed to, especially outside urban areas. It is even lower down on the priority list than doctors, and a visit to the dentist is usually to solve a problem that cannot be solved in another way, such as prolonged use of *raki* to mask the pain.

In the summer the dental profession gets a boost as Albanians who live abroad, recognising the importance of functioning teeth from those around them in their host nations, come back home to have theirs fixed at considerably lower prices than in the countries where they are resident.

Toilet seats

There is a national shortage of toilet seats. This is not because they are outrageously expensive, nor because people prefer to use the porcelain 'squats' which still exist. Neither is there an epidemic of kleptomania where the stolen trophy is hung up proudly on a wall with a description of its original location. No, the flimsy toilet seat attachments are the culprits, and the unused seat remains propped up against the wall or absent altogether. Women don't repair them because 'it's a man's job' and men don't bother because toilet seats are not considered key to their comfort.

Custom & Tradition

The Kanun

No book on Albanians would be complete without mention of the 'Kanun', not because it plays a particularly major role in the lives of today's Albanians, but rather because it underpins many aspects of Albanian life in the past and even the present.

The Kanun is a set of spoken laws, covering most aspects of potential legal disputes, which existed in Central and Northern Albania and the surrounding areas. The most famous codified version was by Lek Dukadjini in the 15th century, repeated by word of mouth and finally written out in the 19th century. It set out the rights and duties of the population and redress in cases of dispute. In the absence of real central authority and a functioning judiciary in these parts, it was the only effective means of legal authority up to communist times.

> **" The 'Kanun' underpins many aspects of Albanian life in the past and even the present. "**

Since communism, it has allegedly made a return, often to fill the vacuum left by lack of central authority. Indeed, some folk are nostalgic for the Kanun as the more socially acceptable parts (for the modern man) emphasise the good of the community over the interests of the individual.

Some parts of the Kanun would strike the reader as exemplary; for example, the resolution of property rights or the rules on hospitality. Others,

> **66 Although most Albanians would shun the notion of blood feud, there is a very strong belief in getting even. 99**

notably the treatment of women as property, would not garner sympathy from even the most hardened of western misogynists. One of the most memorable features, however, is the setting out of when it is justifiable to 'take blood' (*gjakmarre*): in other words, kill someone.

The Kanun states that a life can be taken only to avenge a killing. However, many killings nowadays are done on the basis of the flimsiest of reasons; for example, the killing of women and children which is strictly not allowed under the rules of the Kanun, except in the case of adultery. Albanian criminals often cite the Kanun as an exculpation of their actions, though these actions would not always be permitted according to the rules of the Kanun.

Although most Albanians would shun the notion of blood feud, there is a very strong belief in getting even, creating a balance by righting a wrong, or simply not allowing the other person to think you are a pushover – one of the worst sins of Albanian manhood. As Edith Durham quoted a villager: "You must kill the man that injured you, or he will treat you worse and worse." In this case, often the best form of defence for a wrong is to allow the victim to do what is necessary to restore honour and to avoid letting the rancour linger and get worse. The Albanians have long memories for perceived insults.

Courtship

In days gone by, children were often betrothed at an early age, frequently before they were born, by parents eager to build relations between two families. The happy couple often didn't meet one another until the wedding day which added extra spice to the ceremony. More recently, the bride and groom were selected on the basis of suitability, as if specific criteria were ticked off by the family.

❝ Until recently, even in the large cities, the person you went out with is the person you marry. ❞

Nowadays, both male and female have a greater say in who they marry, although what their parents or the girl's brother want may still play a major role. There is no room for experimenting. Until recently, even in the large cities, the person you went out with is the person you marry. For someone to openly have different partners before finally getting married at best raised eyebrows and at worst caused a scandal.

The traditional courtship ritual went like this: a girl signalled her interest in a boy through subtle, and then less subtle body language. The boy invited the girl to coffee. They were seen together and then, particularly in villages, engagement followed fairly quickly to avoid people scandal-mongering. Even today, the engagement can be a long-drawn-out affair but almost always leads to marriage unless one party dares to call it off and thereby risk family disapproval.

> **❝ Weddings are gargantuan affairs with upwards of 300 people and hoover up the family finances for years to come. ❞**

This ritual is fast becoming a thing of the past, especially in towns, but 'going out with someone' still suggests a rather longer term commitment than would be the case anywhere else.

Weddings

Weddings are gargantuan affairs with upwards of 300 people from the extended family (including second and third cousins that are never likely to meet except at weddings) and hoover up the family finances for years to come. It is, of course, worth it for the bride who has set her heart on the wedding.

The arrangements and the aftermath highlight the complex rules and sensitivities of Albanian society.

Exclusion from the guest list can result in, at least, a tit-for-tat exclusion of not only the person but of that part of the family. The wedding itself can be a thinly disguised powder keg of protocol. During the dancing, certain parts of the family have their rightful time to get up and dance, and of course there is the seating plan to be arranged. In fact, anybody who manages to stage an Albanian wedding without any hitches or arguments certainly has the ability to arrange international peace conferences between nations about to go to war.

Culture

Books

Albanians are avid readers, though mainly of newspapers. While it is common to see men reading newspapers in public places, it is rare to see anybody reading a book, even in student areas. Bookshops are few and far between and do less than a roaring trade, but they doggedly continue to exist despite the obvious economic drawbacks of doing so. Books are also laid out for sale along pavements.

All Albanians are familiar with their nation's writers of the last 100 years, though they may never have read their books. Many works by famous authors were banned during the communist era and disappeared into obscurity. These days, the most famous author is

Ismael Kadare who started writing under communism, and by clever symbolism and allegory was able to present some important social and political issues without being censored.

A number of titles by foreign authors are available in Albanian, though the literary merits of some of the translations are not always apparent.

Children's heroes

Role models, such as *Alice in Wonderland* in the English-speaking world, *Cruel Frederik* for German children and *A witch that eats children* for young Russians, arguably leave a strong impression on a nation's psyche. Albania is similarly rich in legends and folk characters, such as Muji and Halili who smote the foreigners of the north. Such stories have been passed down through generations, but they are now heard less and less as foreign characters take over.

> **66** Albanians are familiar with their nation's writers of the last 100 years, though they may never have read their books. **99**

In communist times, if children were able to tear themselves away from such classics as Enver Hoxha's *Imperialism and Revolution* or *Aspects of the Construction of Socialism in The People's Socialist Republic of Albania,* they could enjoy hearing about young people who resisted the fascist invader, often dying in the process, or be treated to tales of girls throwing themselves onto rocks rather than become slaves of the Turks. More prosaic characters that have left an imprint include Çufo, the pig who told children not to steal and to respect others, and whose song is still remembered by a generation.

> **Albanians easily identify the music of their area as well as sing the songs and follow the dance steps.**

The most famous Albanian hero is Gjergji Kastrioti Skanderbeg who defeated the Ottoman Turks numerous times in battle; and it was said that by keeping the Turks occupied he prevented them from mustering enough soldiers to attack Europe. His statue stands in Tirana's main square, which carries his name.

The second most famous hero is Mother Teresa. She also has a square named after her in Tirana and is widely fêted for being famous throughout the world.

Folk dress and dancing

Folk dress and folk music are concrete symbols of the Albanians' traditions. The variety of regional folk dress, though seldom worn, is still maintained and Albanians easily identify the music of their area as well as sing the songs and follow the dance steps, which they proudly do at weddings.

Folk music is often heard in the media. One TV

channel plays folk music with accompanying dancers, ranging from the almost authentic to the faintly pastiche, with a middle-aged man in a folk jacket holding his arms wide and crooning folk songs, and a row of scantily clad young ladies in various states of folk dress dancing behind him.

Norman who?

To those with a more than passing acquaintance with British films of the 1950s and 1960s, one of the better known western connections with Albanian life is Norman Wisdom, the British comedy actor. He was a favourite of the dictator and his films were therefore allowed to be shown. It was assumed that Norman Wisdom was popular because he portrayed the epitome of the downtrodden worker in capitalist Britain, fighting for rights against an evil employer and ultimately winning, while looked on with sympathy and compassion by beautiful women.

> **66 Albanians are baffled by the interest of foreigners in Norman Wisdom's association with Albania. 99**

Albanians are baffled by the interest of foreigners in Norman Wisdom's association with Albania. The young are unlikely to have seen the films and therefore have no idea who he is, while those in the know are aware of him as Mr Pitkin, his film character, rather than (Sir) Norman Wisdom.

That he isn't considered a hero alongside Skanderbeg and Mother Theresa is due to his having no claim whatsoever to Albanian ancestry and to his film character being bumbling, humble, self-effacing, kind to animals, constantly in the wrong and apologetic – the very antithesis of what an Albanian man should be. And he did not have a car.

Systems

Transport

Albanians have an almost infinite number of ways to travel across the country: bus, minibus, car, motorcycle, moped, train, bicycle, taxi and foot. If you sub-categorise the list to public transport, the list is reduced to bus, minibus and train. And taxi.

The train service is a fairly basic affair which can lay claim to being the most challenged in Europe. Railways are single track, on which trains occasionally come and go. They are not fast: in fact, young boys like to race them and win, and farmers have time to shoo their sheep off the track when they see the train coming. The signalling equipment along the lines has long since disappeared, no doubt fulfilling useful alternative needs.

66 Railways are single track, on which trains occasionally come and go. 99

The greatest advantage of train travel is that it is cheap but the downside is the lack of investment. Some folk like to stand at the side of the track and throw stones at the windows of the train as it passes by. The broken windows afford a welcome form of air conditioning in hot weather, but are annoying when it rains. There are also plenty of vacant seats to choose from.

Buses are marginally faster and are more crowded than trains. They tend to run on time, whereas minibuses, in various states of

66 Minibuses do not run to schedule; rather, they depart when they are full. 99

disrepair, do not run to schedule; rather, they depart when they are full. 'Full' does not mean that all the seats and upturned buckets are occupied; 'Albanian full' is when every available space is used up, including standing room, and just when you think it is impossible to fit in anybody else, a further four passengers and their belongings will be shoe-horned in, adapting their bodies to the shape of the spaces between the other bodies.

As the minibus speeds its way down the road, the eagle-eyed driver might spot a pedestrian who shows a vague interest in the bus by raising an eyebrow. This prompts the driver to brake violently in the hope of procuring yet another passenger. Fortunately those inside the bus are cushioned from any real damage caused by the extreme braking by the fact that there are lots of soft bodies to fall against, rather like human shock absorbers.

The media

For a small country, Albania has a surprising number of TV channels and newspapers. In theory, this should give rise to a plurality of views. In fact, as many of them rely on advertising revenue from companies which themselves are heavily dependent on government patronage (and indeed the final ownership of the media is not always clear), ultimately the views reflect those of the three major parties. This means, in effect, they either support the government or don't support the government, and the editorial is a sort of post-hoc rationalisation of the position of the party it supports.

> **66 Discussion means who can get their point across more often and in a louder voice. 99**

Much of the printed media is dedicated to domestic politics and much of radio and TV is devoted to discussion of politics. As discussion means who can get their point across more often and in a louder voice, the point of the topic is lost and the emphasis is on being right and scoring points, all at the same time. Fortunately, on television it is possible to see who is saying what by lip reading and matching the voices to the speakers; whereas on radio, the listener is treated to an orgy of loud opinion, rather like a badly synchronised verbal orchestra, rising slowly towards a crescendo of mutual recrimination.

Television

Italian television has had a major influence on Albanians. When the number of Italian TV stations increased following the de-monopolisation of Italian state television in the late 1970s, it became almost impossible for the communist authorities to jam all of them, but it was still considered a seditious offence to watch them.

Many Albanians have become cosmopolitan through the simple expedient of total immersion in soap operas ('telenovela') imported from Latin America and Turkey. This has meant that, in addition to good Italian and a smattering of other languages, young people have a fair knowledge of Spanish. In the absence of any other external influence, Albanians began to copy the decor and clothes more suited to São Paolo than Shkoder. It was the new reality, and divorces shot up as Albanian wives started to compare their husbands to glamorous and charming Carlos or Eduardo who became the new benchmarks for husbands and for family life.

> **66 Albanians have become cosmopolitan through the simple expedient of total immersion in soap operas. 99**

Some Albanians have a curious worldliness where, for example, they may be fully conversant with all aspects of the Feraz family tree from prolonged exposure to a particular Brazilian soap opera and have more than a vague understanding of Brazilian Portuguese, but they would be hard put to identify where Rio de Janeiro is on the world map.

Education

Albanians generally agree that educational standards have slipped somewhat in the last 20 years. Many parents have come to believe that the key to success is to encourage schoolteachers to award their child high marks, or the students to persuade the lecturer to help them pass the exam by whatever means possible, or whatever price is appropriate.

> **66 What outsiders may call cheating in exams is called 'helping others to get round the system'. 99**

The practice has become so institutionalised that there are teachers who suggest the child takes extra private classes with them (for a fee, of course) if they are to have 'any hope of passing their exams'. This is true of both private and state schools. In their endeavours to get a qualification rather than an education, what outsiders may call cheating in exams is called 'helping others to get round the system' and therefore is fully justified.

Albania has over 40 universities. For a population of about three million, this suggests that Albanians are very studious. The vast majority of universities are private, and some have very low student numbers. When lack of proper monitoring led to a situation where a university issued a diploma to an overseas student who had apparently never set foot in Albania, many claimed this was not an isolated case.

66 There is a belief that the higher the status in society a person has, the less they feel the rules apply to them. 99

There are moves to rationalise the universities and somehow monitor standards. However, the heady cocktail of many people's expectations and vested interests makes this a thorny issue to address.

Law & Order

Albanians generally adhere tenuously to rules. Smoking is banned in bars and restaurants and many have signs to that effect. However, bar owners suspect that if they never turned an occasional blind eye to its enforcement, they would have no customers and therefore no longer a bar in which to hang the sign.

There is a belief that the higher the status in society a person has, the less they feel the rules apply to them. In fact, breaking the rules is a '*droit de seigneur*', or one of the privileges of rank. This carries through into many aspects of society – a person driving a very big or expensive car claims more right than anyone in charge of a smaller car to drive off when the traffic lights are still red, or park on the pavement, or in front of the emergency entrance to the hospital.

As in all countries, diplomats are generally immune from prosecution for traffic offences, but in Albania foreigners may be too, if the offence is not too extreme. Local offenders can frequently talk their way out, possibly with some financial offering, and even when clearly in the wrong will feel inclined to argue. While a 'No' in many countries signals the end of the discussion, in Albania it can herald the beginning of a negotiation – with the police or anybody else. In fact, where there are rules, there are negotiations.

> **While a 'No' in many countries signals the end of the discussion, in Albania it can herald the beginning of a negotiation.**

Corruption

Any foreigner, inside or outside Albania, will cite corruption as one of the malaises of Albanian society. Albanians agree that corruption is a bad thing. When pressed, however, it's actually other people's corruption, not their own, that is the problem. Theirs is not really corruption; it's a certain sort of wrong-doing tempered by the fact that they have to survive in a difficult environment.

Besides, goes the logic, one single person avoiding corruption will not spell the end of a corrupt society as everybody else will still continue to be involved in it. And therein lies the crux. To be seen not to be taking advantage of a situation when it is presented to you would label you as naïve. Or it may elicit the sarcastic comment: '*Ai eshte shume ndershem*' (Oh, he's *very* honest). In any case, if you refuse to take advantage of something corrupt when it's presented to you, people will not believe you are being honest but will be convinced you are taking advantage of the situation in a more clever way; that you are being even more corrupt, giving rise to the comment: 'He behaves as if he's honest.' They just can't see exactly how.

> **❝ From time to time, posters appear in the streets, exhorting the population to 'Fight corruption'. ❞**

There is no clear consensus on what corruption is. From time to time, posters appear in the streets, exhorting the population to 'Fight corruption' as though everybody knows what they are fighting against.

Albanians are very tolerant when they see clear cases of corruption, despite the efforts of those who recognise the damage it does to the economy and society. Where a politician is caught on camera apparently bribing somebody and it is broadcast on television, the reaction is not one of righteous indignation but a careless shrug of the shoulders and the comment,

❝ One's first loyalty is to family and friends and to repaying moral debts. ❞

'We know it goes on, so it's not a surprise'. Low expectations by the population of their politicians gives the latter licence to commit all sorts of misdeeds. There is even an expectation that high office holders will take advantage of their positions to commit acts of corruption, which is what many people in their situation would doubtless do.

In a society where one's first loyalty is to family and friends and to repaying moral debts, helping society in general or obeying the rules of society or government comes further down the hierarchy of obligations. Some Albanians claim that outsiders have never really understood the concept of 'family and friends first', with the result that foreign money earmarked for the public good has disappeared, to re-emerge in the form of private villas, fast cars, or holidays for the family.

Counterfeits

Albanians feel justified in buying a cheaper copy of a luxury brand article, such as a handbag, by complaining that the original is too expensive. Indeed, some will argue that it is better value for money to buy the cheaper version. Thus, shops and markets have large supplies of counterfeit products. Even Western books are republished in Albania without permission. If the lawyer bringing the case could be sure of full support from the courts, Albania would be an intellectual property lawyer's paradise.

Government & Business

Albanian connections

Relationships between people in northern Europe are generally transparent and clear. In Albania they are complicated and opaque.

To illustrate this with telegraph poles: in developed countries, electrical wires pass from pole to pole in a neat, ordered and visible fashion connecting people and properties. Albanian telegraph poles have jumbles of wires arranged in complex and apparently random overlap – some hanging in mid air – as a result of requisite connections meet-

❝ In Albania relationships are complicated and opaque. ❞

ing different needs at different times. The extraordinary thing is that everybody has an electrical connection and these connections generally work (unless somebody in the Power-Central decides to cut the power or there is a malfunction in the central generator).

Relationships between the boss and the subordinate are meshed together in the same messy but effective manner. Lines of communication are the result of kinship, friendships over many years, favours given personally or by relatives in a way that not even the recipient may necessarily be able to rationalise. Often at work, a worker will help another colleague not because that is their job, but because they are doing them a favour and therefore can expect one in return.

Politics

As in business, so in politics. Political office and the political administration have been filled with people who have the jobs as a result of returned favours and obligations of family and friends. To consider this corrupt is to misunderstand the real moral imperatives that operate in Albania. If a minister in the government does not give his brother the job that he has asked for, he

> **If a minister does not give his brother the job he has asked for, he will be 'persona non grata' at the next family get-together.**

will be 'persona non grata' at the next family get-together. In this sense, therefore, not helping a member of your family to get a job, avoid a fine, get a coveted place at a university would signal the beginning of a breakdown in the family values as they are known and enjoyed in Albania.

In general, people do not rate the government or the instruments of power very highly. This is partly because parliamentary debate is reduced to personal criticism, and the opposition feels that its role is... well, just to oppose. This happens to such an extent that both governments and opposition parties are characteristically devoid of any proper manifesto or strategy which means there is a total absence of consensus on any issue.

Despite this, Albanians duly go to the polls at election time and vote. Their job may be safe with a specific party, or they may have been promised an administration job with the new party. In the meantime, many dream of getting away and working abroad. Others stay and get on with life, or leave and then return home with the genuine wish to improve government and society. But galvanising support for active grass roots reform tends to dissipate when sitting in a café discussing it, and accumulating theoretical coffee units.

> **" Opposition parties are characteristically devoid of any proper manifesto or strategy which means there is a total absence of consensus on any issue. "**

Freedom and democracy

During Hoxha's time, the state tried to regulate every aspect of people's lives. Since then, by political conviction or lack of competence, or possibly a combination of both, successive governments have tended to favour a laissez-faire approach, leaving the populace very much to their own devices in matters of disputes, traffic control, education and most other things.

Although communism ended in 1991, its shadow still looms heavily, and in many ways it is as if the last 20 years have not existed. This sentiment is perhaps encouraged by some politicians who prefer to compare the current situation with communist times, rather than draw their citizens' attention to the unsteady progress of the country so far.

> **66 Successive governments have tended to favour a laissez-faire approach, leaving the populace very much to their own devices. 99**

Everything that used to be praised – communal effort, hard work, order, discipline and a collective belief in a messianic vision – is perceived as being part and parcel of Hoxha's communist repression. In contrast, 'democracy' represents individualism, leisure, disorder, indiscipline and, for many, a belief in self-interest and indifference to the world outside the family.

If a driver cannot find a parking space on the road, he parks on the pavement, thus blocking the path of a woman with a pushchair. A house owner may extend his house to cover part or all of the pavement, or a bar owner may cover the pavement with tables and chairs, forcing pedestrians to walk in the road. A stretch of magnificent scenery is spoilt because somebody builds a house so that he can be in the middle of it. He cannot see how this has blotted out the countryside for everybody else because he is inside, delighting in the view.

The economy

The economy is currently deemed to be one of the poorest-performing in Europe. The country produces very little in the way of manufactured goods, and its raw materials are exported to be processed and branded abroad. In 25 years Albania has moved from painful self-sufficiency to economic dependence on imported goods.

Albania is almost unique amongst European nations in that much of its income is derived from a Albanians working abroad. With most products being imported, and the money that comes into the country from abroad via relatives being used to buy these imported goods,

> **66 Albania is, at best, only a temporary transit stay for foreign money. 99**

the money goes straight back to the producing countries. Thus Albania is, at best, only a temporary transit stay for foreign money.

Economic and therefore political dissatisfaction over the years has been muted because many people enjoy the trappings of consumerism which would not be possible without remittances from abroad.

Professions

In communist times, the state decided young people's professions according to the needs of the economy. Later the parents or grandparents chose the profession of the children. Now, younger people tend to decide for themselves and are opting for attractive, high-status professions. As a result, there is a surfeit of graduates in law and economics and a shortage of suitably qualified electricians, carpenters and construction workers. Indeed, many parents would rather say that their child is an unemployed law graduate than a busy and successful plumber.

> **❝ In a business deal Albanians will be determined not to let you get one over on them. ❞**

When a student is asked 'What sort of job do you want to have?', the answer will be invariably: 'a manager'. A 'manager' is perceived as one who drives an impressive car, wears smart suits, owns expensive gadgets, has an office and the freedom to bark orders at others. Many graduates become rapidly disillusioned that they cannot reach these heady heights in a short space of time, and seek to try their hand abroad where they believe they can.

Win the battle, lose the war

In a business deal Albanians will be determined not to let you get one over on them and will therefore not yield an inch. Hence, a landlord will proudly proclaim that although his flat has been empty for 12 months, he held firm with potential tenants by not being prepared to lower his price when they tried to negotiate a 5% discount. This taught them that they weren't dealing with a pushover. The fact that he had lost a year's earnings was less important than being seen as a tough negotiator. As in other areas of life, it is more important to win the immediate battle than the overall war.

The boss is king

The contractual relationship found in most Western countries between employer and employee, where rights and duties are set out and are largely treated as sacrosanct, does not really exist for Albanians. If the boss suddenly decides that the employee has to stay late to finish a job or to work on a job he was not specifically employed for, it is the employee's duty to do it. The relationship may at times resemble serfdom.

> **The relationship between boss and employee may at times resemble serfdom.**

The touching of forelocks is largely invisible but is communicated by language: some bosses actually prefer to be called '*Shef*' – Boss. A *Shef* doesn't delegate; when a project has to be implemented. Rather than pool ideas, allocate responsibilities and agree timings, the *Shef* will try to do it all himself and give subordinates tasks on an ad hoc basis. This ensures that the

Shef is fully in control but allows for a plethora of mistakes to be made. Of course, if the employees are aware of this they would do better than to point it out. The boss's word is law even, or rather, most particularly, when he is wrong.

In large or state organisations, where an employee may have friends, relatives or contacts who are more powerful than the boss, the actual line of authority is more blurred and the standard levers of bosses do not apply. Real authority is not defined by legal or organisational norms but by who holds the reins of power.

Language

Many Albanians will proudly boast how difficult their language is. According to them the difficulty lies not in the post positional articles, or the optative or admirative moods, but in the fact that Albanian has 36 letters. On closer inspection, you find that approximately 25% of them are two letters put together, such as 'dh' and 'th' and 'sh'. It's almost as if, in competing in the Olympic Alphabet Race, the Albanian team doubled up the letters in an attempt to win gold.

For the lingo-learner there are specific difficulties. One is the fact that Albanians will almost always try to talk in English or Italian to a foreigner, either as an act of hospitality or to practise their own language skills. Another is the wide range of regional dialects and accents. This is as tricky for Albanians. If you grew up in Tirana, you have to relearn

> **66 What you think is a cucumber – a *kastravec* – may turn out to be a *trangull* or even a *sallator*. 99**

when going to other parts of Albania. Indeed, you may not need to venture out of Tirana at all, as the man you buy the phonecard from hails from Çameria, the man who cuts your hair is from Korce, and the baker comes from the North. What you think is a cucumber – a *kastravec* – may turn out to be a *trangull* or even a *sallator*, depending on the regional origins of the person you are buying from.

It doesn't matter, Albanians are comfortable in a world where complete mutual comprehension is absent.

Some nifty maxims

He wants to get fat from a flea (he wants to get blood from a stone).

The fish in the sea, the pan in the fire. (Don't count your chickens before they hatch).

When the lion is not there, the monkey becomes king.

He has hung the liver from the wolf's neck. (He has chosen a dangerous option.)

A word is like a bee, it can produce honey but it can also sting.

If you want to know what the family is hiding, ask the child. If you want to know what is in a man's soul, give him *raki*.

Conversation

Gossip

The nation's major source of amusement is the discomfort or criticism of others, and people will readily join in a conversation to shred the reputation of a friend or acquaintance, preferably if it can lead to hoots of mirth or give the speakers a moment of superiority in this hostile world.

As people are paranoid that they might be being laughed at, one way of mitigating this fear is to do the same to others. So gossiping is a defence mechanism – 'Talk about others before they talk about you.'

Greetings

A chance encounter in the street with a friend is not the occasion for a quick nod or a hello. For Albanians there is no tentative, half-hearted greeting. To all but the most complete strangers, the full battery of conversation is used and goes something like this:

– How are you?
– Well.
– And the family?
– Well.
– And your parents?
– Well.
– And work?
– Well.
– And your health?
– Well. And how are you?
– I'm well.
– So, you're well?
– Really well.
– So, everything's well?
– Very well.
– I'm glad everything's well.
– What are you doing now?
– Nothing.
– Nothing?
– Nothing.

And so it continues. If you are upset that your work colleague has been promoted over your head, or your child has just married someone with no connections or '*perspektive*' (prospects) or you have suspected symptoms of beriberi, it's all good – and you are well.

The Author

Alan Andoni spent his formative years in England, Northern Ireland and Scotland. His interest in all things Albanian began in the 1970s as a dedicated listener of foreign radio broadcasts. Radio Tirana was a particular favourite for its surreal, but stirring narrative.

Visits to Albania over the years have convinced him that there is an allure which is both positive and infectious to anybody who spends any significant time there. He finds he has developed an aversion to microplanning, a yearning for spontaneity and a tendency to commit random acts of kindness. He also tries to multi-task, but as a Northern European male, he still can't quite manage it.

Grateful thanks are given to friends for their contributions to this guide, in particular:

Bato Bega, Enriko Ceko, Mark Cholij, Edmond Ibrahimi, Elisa Isufaj, Jonela Kuro, Ina Lulaj, Pamela Qafoku and Vasil Shpata.

Xenophobe's® guides

Available as printed books and e-books:

The Albanians	The Italians
The Americans	The Japanese
The Aussies	The Kiwis
The Austrians	The Norwegians
The Belgians	The Poles
The Canadians	The Portuguese
The Chinese	The Russians
The Czechs	The Scots
The Danes	The Swedes
The Dutch	The Swiss
The English	The Welsh
The Estonians	
The Finns	
The French	**Xenophobe's®**
The Germans	**lingo learners**
The Greeks	German
The Icelanders	Greek
The Irish	Italian
The Israelis	Spanish

Xenophobe's Guides

The Americans

 The American language embraces the bias towards good feelings. Stocks that plummet to half their value aren't losers, they're 'non-performers'. Someone doesn't have a near brush with death; he or she has a 'life-affirming experience'.

The Italians

 Most of Italian life is spent in public, on show, and Italians know the importance of *bella figura* (cutting a fine figure). Because ordinary Italian life is lived on stage, Italian theatre often looks as if it is overacted – it has to be, to differentiate it from the high drama of real life.

The Austrians

 As a result of the languages and intelligence of several peoples being gathered into a unity, the Austrians live in several diverse traditions and are thus capable of taking up different positions simultaneously.

The English

Tradition, to the English, represents continuity, which must be preserved at all costs. It gives them a sense of permanence in an age of change. Like a well-worn jersey with holes in the sleeves, it's the comfort of the familiar.

The Greeks

The ancient sages carved 'Nothing in excess' and 'Know thyself' on the portals of the Delphic Oracle in an attempt to persuade their fellow Greeks to curb their emotions. They were not heeded then any more than they are now.

The Germans

The Germans strongly disapprove of the irrelevant, the flippant, the accidental. On the whole Germans would prefer to forgo a clever invention rather than admit that creativity is a random and chaotic process.

Xenophobe's® Guides e-books are available from Amazon, iBookstore, and other online sources, and via:

www.xenophobes.com

Xenophobe's® Guides print versions can be purchased through online retailers (Amazon, etc.) or via our web site:

www.xenophobes.com

Xenophobe's® Guides are pleased to offer a quantity discount on book orders. Why not embellish an occasion – a wedding goody bag, a conference or other corporate event – with our guides. Or treat yourself to a full set of the paperback edition. Ask us for details:

Xenophobe's® Guides

telephone: +44 (0)20 7733 8585
e-mail: info@xenophobes.com

Xenophobe's® Guides enhance your understanding of the people of different nations. Don't miss out – order your next Xenophobe's® Guide soon.

Xenophobe's Guides